Previous Books by Julia B. Levine

Ordinary Psalms (LSU Press 2021). Nautilus Award.
Small Disasters Seen in Sunlight (LSU Press 2014). Winner of the 2015 Northern California Book Award in Poetry.
Ditch-tender (University of Tampa Press 2007).
Ask, 2000 Tampa Review Prize for Poetry (University of Tampa Press 2003).
Practicing for Heaven, 1998 Anhinga Prize for Poetry, selected by Enid Shomer (Anhinga Press 1999).

Lullaby for the Sixth Extinction

Lullaby for the Sixth Extinction

Julia B. Levine

Wolfson Press
2025

Designed by Sky Santiago.
 First edition.

ISBN: 978-1-950066-25-4

Wolfson Press
Master of Liberal Studies Program
Indiana University South Bend
1700 Mishawaka Avenue
South Bend, Indiana 46634-7111
WolfsonPress.com

Contents

Foreword

The question of how we reconcile nature's astounding beauty and its unflinching indifference to suffering is one that surfaces when reading the exquisite poems in Julia B. Levine's *Lullaby for the Sixth Extinction*. In an early poem, "How It Begins," the speaker wakes in the night only to hear a coyote eating a heron; she listens to its "broken singing." Death is imminent and inevitable, but that doesn't mean we won't call out its cruelty, or rage against life's unfairness, or plead with an absent God. The story within these pages is heartbreaking: her infant grandson has cancer. She's a witness to his chemo treatments, his fight for life in the ICU, and his stay in the pediatric oncology ward. Unfair, indeed.

She breaks away from the madness and finds respite in the natural world—its beauty—and her faith in its ability to restore hope. How would one live without staying alert to lush fields where "earth cracked open into yellow bells // tiny velvet cups" or "striped lacewings dip in and out of purple wands"? But here's the catch: humans are destroying the very planet that sustains them (the earth's sixth extinction is man-made). Another question: If the grandson survives, isn't he entitled to experience nature's pleasures and abundances? One of her many strengths is juxtaposing the sterile hospital room and its cold machinery with California landscapes teeming with life. Or not, since some of it has been or is being destroyed by drought and other catastrophic events. "It's hard to love what may die / too soon," she asserts in the title poem.

At the start of the same poem, we encounter a gorgeous metaphor and dazzling sound:

> In the purgatory of whatever paradise remains,
>   I wish for my daughter's call
>
> in my garden after rain, the sun a lit match
>   held to the gas stove of spring,
>
> daffodils sizzling yellow, the swell of tulips
>   shoved through ground.

Her argument with God morphs and multiplies as she moves through this harrowing experience. Time slows as she waits, helpless to do anything that will ease her grandson's suffering. In "Midsummer Argument with Fester & Rot," she makes a symbolic gesture by saving a starling chick that has fallen from its nest even though its chance for survival is impossible. She wonders whether she should interfere. "[W]ho am I to mess / with the merciless machinery of this world?" she asks. These poems take you straight into that merciless machinery. When you emerge, just possibly you might love the world more. *More* says the baby—his first word—as he walks joyfully on "his new legs" into a precarious future. On our walk toward that same future, let's bring Levine's poems along with us.

Nancy Botkin
South Bend, Indiana

Lullaby for the Sixth Extinction

Milk

Even in the dream, it's long past possible
when I uncover my breast and hold the baby
close to drink. How helpless he is,

helpless as the mind in a deep dream
to stop and change direction. Though, on waking,
the mind remembers our grown daughters

and the room where we sleep, and beyond it,
the outside made white with smoke from a fire.
Remembers yesterday's eerie, milk-gold light

we walked through. Then stopped beside
a baby fox. Wasps lit on his skull,
their black bodies beading his torn torso,

while gnats and flies sipped at the glistening.
And the work of those winged things was a fire
chewing through manzanita and alder,

Douglas fir and cedar; the maggots and flies
and wasps carrying the forest out of the fox,
the way the fire carries the forest out of the world.

You asked if a mother fox could feel sadness.
And because last night my mind had used a memory
of my body to deceive me, had pressed our son close,

believing if he drank, I could keep him, today
I want to believe the dead fox was a twin,
a mirror image following behind, the way

a dream can shadow the mind, and the mind
helpless against our stillborn son who lives inside
my dreams and runs silent as a wild fox

behind our daughters. It was almost dusk
when we turned to go, so quickly the wasps and flies
rose together, as if the black and yellow robe

they wore in the milk-gold light had slipped
from the death they were covering. All of us helpless
against the beauty of the troubled world as it burns.

I.

...Dark inkling
it was, to the nether world
of the minor key.
The dead
lean forward.

—Marianne Boruch

Second Coming

Our family's faith died long ago, though it's God
my daughter damns to hell, leaning across the guardrail

of the hospital's rooftop garden, before letting me
curl around her on the ground where she lies.

Last night when the nurse found my daughter sobbing,
she said, *At your son's wedding, this will be a story that you tell.*

And yet, inside the ICU, my grandson, in a white crib,
bleeds into his brain, with no one to explain his whimper,

his erratic heartrate, the little melody of matter
he will always sing in me. No one but the night doctor

mumbling that our boy might die. Still, let's say he lives.
That one day I'll tell him how his grandfather, his aunt and I

lay down on dirt beside his mother, our faces turned up
to rain, a darkening grey. We listened to helicopters taking off,

their roaring like angels come to rid the evening of its wolves.
Hours dragged through a black to whitening sky.

When we walked back inside, wet and cold, we huddled
around my grandson's crib as if to warm our hands at a fire.

And then the story of his second coming.
This happened so long ago, I'll begin. *It was once upon a time.*

How It Begins

At first a rumble, then thunder cracks apart the morning
and suddenly I remember half-waking last night

to a heron shrieking
as a coyote made a meal of stilts and feathers—

though in my stupor, I misheard it as drunken boys
yelling *Hooray!* slowly over and over again,

as if death was jubilant,
with a broken singing in his mouth.

Last August when my daughter birthed her first child,
force and counterforce wrestled in the mystery

of her body and its absence still occupying mine.
Today lighting welds four forks of vanishing

into a sky that has, overnight, lost a bit of winged blue.
There, further out along the brambled roadside,

I remember last summer,
blackberries scattered behind a trio of women

as they carried their overfilled buckets home.
And thinking then, *This baby will destroy the whole of her.*

I should know. Speak to me of love and I'll answer ruin
begins as a brimming sweetness, threatening to spill.

On the Carrizo Plains

Begin again, but ferociously,
something decades old has decreed

in this technicolor overwhelm,
its after-rain and heat, floor-to-ceiling glory.

As if to tame the super-bloom,
I name the showy minutes,

Owl clover, penstemon, baby blue eyes,
California poppies, lupine.

Under a blue salt sky, for a while,
my thoughts lean north

where my grandson sleeps,
his last round of chemo

dripping into a central line, his tiny chest
a bullseye in my mind

where I've stowed him beside me
in the marrow of such extravagance,

and yes,
his fingers tear the sepals up from dirt,

stuff petals into his mouth.
Because even if it's brief,

he's hungry
for the world that he's been given.

So I keep repeating, as I do,
Clover, penstemon, baby blue eyes.

Meaning, if he lives.
If he can be carried through.

Children's Oncology Floor

It's so quiet that a baby crying down the hall
resembles music. And so too the uncommon beauty

of this pigeon perched on a steel girder eight floors up,
her marbled brown and white wings folded down,

before she rises over rooftops, out to San Francisco Bay.
And I want that bird to fly deep into yesterday,

where my grandson is simply a baby with a mouthful
of plastic keys and a mobile of bright stars and moons

singing its way around his head. And I want the pigeon
to drop a note down to the prayer ladies posted outside

the hospital chapel, the paper printed with his full name,
Roger Steven Hansen, so the faithful can beseech on his behalf,

believing however it is they do, that God's will be done
with a Broviac catheter and feeding tube and caustic chemo

excreted into diapers changed every hour as his new body
burns from the inside out. And because I can only watch

so long, I sit awhile outside his room, listening to Chopin
float down the hall from the nurses' station.

Wondering what it is, like music, that bridges one moment
to the next. Then this child in a bright pink dress and hat

turns the corner. She and her mother wheel an IV pole
between them. *Great job, Honey,* her mom says,

as the girl's skeletal legs step haltingly across the floor.
Surrender will be the last thing I have left.

But for now let this child walk out of her grave,
showing us how slowly, deliberately, it must be done.

Little Vamp

Little Vamp, we call him. Twice a week,
a bag of red blood cells hangs on his IV pole.

Blood-lover, we tease. His heart wired
to the monitor's neon green.

Usually, I hold him at the window
so he can bang his stacking cups on glass,

but he has kept nothing down
for close to a week. His parents rarely leave

this room. I try not to think about God,
the petty bigshot, or why our pale grandson

in his metal crib has spent most of his life
inside. Outside, he screams at sunlight.

Today his third round of chemo drips
into his chest. *Let's dress him up as a vampire*

for Halloween, my daughter joked last night,
looking at her baby's snow-white skin,

his too-thin body beneath the sheets.
Though it's only spring, why not plan

to costume this boy as death's employee
on a holiday that celebrates the in-between?

Like a middle finger held up to God
and Satan both, all those ghosts and ghouls

stopping for every sweet. Because
an eternity is how long this takes.

Little vamp, because he can't live
without sucking down a few bags of blood.

This is how death hangs around forever.
Ask my daughter if she can sleep.

Inventory of Infant Leukemia

No one talks about terror on the cancer ward,
nor the bored immorality of death,

only white lies to fatten hope.
Only last night's prom down the hall,

bald teens in suits and gowns whirling IV poles
beneath a glitter ball. A girl slow dancing

with her walker, one leg lost to sarcoma.
Nurses, parents, weeping as they watch,

explaining, *These are tears of joy.* On the bardo
of this floor, no one speaks the name of names,

the end of days, the half year of hours shoveled
like dead birds into the furnace's metal drawer.

No one mentions midnight, its grim despair,
or questions who am I to promise my daughter

her son will be fine if she steps outside
for air. So she goes through dim hallways

past ghosts folding their charts into origami cranes,
walks down to the port, the sea lapping over stairs

made of stone. Soon she'll give the wind
the last strand of his hair, white as sunlight.

The paper cranes blow about as litter.
Cargo ships wait to be emptied of their loads.

While Baby Percy Begins Dying

In the room next door, I remember
the seven last things Jesus said
as nurses and doctors gown up, enter, leave.

When I hear sobbing, I revise the first—
Forgive them, they know not what they do—
to include God, given that Percy was just beginning

to talk, learning that words could bring the world to him.
And the second, *Today you will be with me in paradise,*
Percy on his way into wind or water,

or that Korean dogwood in the park,
pale blossoms floating
like delicate saucers brimmed with cream.

Then the third, *Behold the mother, behold the son*,
which must be the one body they share
suffering chemo, radiation, surgeries.

Twelve times Percy's neuroblastoma recurs.
So the fourth, *My God, my God,*
why have You forsaken me?

And the fifth too, *I thirst.*
Meaning, not simply the parch of dying,
but the fierce yearning for a moment more of Percy—

his brown curls, his lilting voice,
that one afternoon he shrieked with joy
in a wheelchair his father raced down the hall.

Now, a loud commotion, footsteps.
The sixth, *It is finished.* Though not quite,
as the family travels past our room

carrying Percy home to die. To surrender
to the last words spoken, Jesus said,
Father, into your hands I place my spirit.

Jesus. If you think there is anything holy
about a baby beginning at the end,
while I lean against this steel crib,

my hand on my grandson's chest
just to feel it empty and fill—
think again.

Questions From the Pediatric Patients

It's dark in this corner of the hall
where I've stepped out of the room to cry.

Death arrives, picks his favorite letters
from the pocket of his robe.

Explains, *They're all different ages,*
these kids with all their questions.

See, this boy was at least sixteen,
and with his eyes closed, Death recites,

"Why do you always arrive at night,
as if chasing a fix like an addict at a trash fire?"

He unfolds another wadded paper.
Reads, *"Did God get to choose first on everything?"*

"Does the soul go fast like smoke
or hang around the room awhile?"

"If I don't die from cancer,
will you be happy, or will you cry?"

Here Death pulls out a ragged hankie
to wipe his eyes. Crazy to see

how Death misses each child.
This one kills me, he says, *a six-year-old*

writing for her dying twin, and reads,
"If you make the wrong one dead

by accident, can you make her
alive again inside our mom?"

Easier Said Than Done

To stay inside it here, where the sky balances
over the bridge joining this borrowed cottage

to the cancer ward. Or driving across the bay
to launder blankets stained with misery—

his plush jubilate gone dark as radio silence.
My mind like a goldfish swimming laps

inside a too-small bowl. My thoughts
circling liver failure and mucositis

and heart damage until I've lapsed into
a loosening of grief, yellow as a finch

flinging herself into the privet. And sings.
Even now, in my nightgown, in the shadow

of my grandson's suffering, I stand
on the cold slate of the balcony staring up

at evening visible through two apple trees,
as elation's sudden helium lifts me between soil

and stars. Brief, but for the moment's span,
I can believe one day love will find him

nearly grown. In a garden like this,
the gate unlatched. Helpless to stop,

he's walking out under jasmine
into the merciless perfume of this world.

Almond Orchard in Blossom

On the way home from the hospital,
I pull off I-80. Seagulls circle

above the trees and I wonder
if entering one world,

then another,
is all the living can do.

As for the dead
pacing the orchard's deepest row,

I want them to know this evening
I will sit beside my grandson's crib again,

parsing the parable of spring—
the earth cracked open into yellow bells,

tiny velvet cups, fierce green buds.
I'll bend my head beside him,

his breath a memory of the orchard
scented with bees and wind.

Perhaps spring is beauty's shatter
and the parable is about breaking apart

the whole of being
into moments, each one drawn down

to a terrifying sweetness.
The way last night, I reached through the bars

of my grandson’s crib,
and though he was still asleep,

his hand curled around my finger,
held me there.

After His Last Chemo, I Visit a Lavender Farm

August and quail hurry though the stubble.
Once, a deer disappearing into woods. At dusk,

fog floats in, darkening the path back home.
When I reach the lavender fields, striped lacewings

dip in and out of purple wands
trembling the flowers, hummingbird moths

with their soft jeweled bodies,
that perfect mimic of dive and hover, whir and hum.

I was not even trying to believe in this world.
But here it seems that everywhere

a moth lets her dark tongue down,
a cup of nectar has been waiting all along.

II.

Listen while I talk on
against time

—William Carlos Williams

Too Late Pastoral

What light did to the day
    could still startle us—sky and field and marsh
    shot through with sun. Especially in late winter,

too late really, to be heading
    into the park, but we did, we knew the trail,
    the granitic cliffs red and rising straight up from sand,

the sea turning molten. We stood
    for an hour and watched the surf knock
    at a heron's thin silhouette, gusts tossing her crest-feathers.

It was good then to walk back
    in the near dark, through the almost gone hills
    and fields. Almost too late, so we stayed to watch

the land hold the vanishing,
    last summer's star thistles bowed in wind, a felt sense
    of animals waiting for the last of our kind to leave.

If Math Might Hold the Terror Down

Just outside the nurses' station, at every shift change
my grandson's cancer maps a geographical territory

on a white board in black erasable marker
& milliliters of milk & numbers of diapers
& bright pink bags of chemo

between naps & loudspeaker codes
we learn to decipher—pink for stolen baby,
blue for heart attack, red for mass shooter.

Every minute measured & yet it startles
how every day vanishes whole

though the hours must be opening correctly somewhere else—

maybe a city park with babies under trees in wind,
a cricket outside the coffee shop singing in time to a concerto.

Sometimes I drive out to Land's End
& stand on the sandstone cliffs above the sea

to be reminded of larger griefs—

our planet in trouble with nitrogen & carbon,
the St Lucia racer snake down to 20,
bluebird of paradise subtracted along with glacial ice.

In this year of maybe-not,
maybe all that saves us

is the way we know to count
the endangered species (near 700 now),

because everywhere my grandson's red circuitry goes
death trails like an understudy,
death in the calendar, death pixelated
in every text my daughter sends.

As if a negative number had escaped, visceral and uncaged
& shadowing every hour—

even today, months after he's left the hospital,
all plump & babbling at his weekly outpatient visit,

the doctor laughing at his antics
(& squawking with excitement, the baby pulls plastic purple gloves
from a box one by one)

until she reads his lab-work & time sparks
sputters out.

This is how it started a year ago:
his blood counted and sorted,
hemoglobin & neutrophils too low,

time breaking down,

the doctor saying, *Don't worry, it's probably nothing,*

time snagged on death's barbed & shaky read
of light's errand,

time refusing to move on.

Stages of Grief

Tattered, sun-dead, there was no river everywhere
I looked. There was dust, whole forests of sun-
burned reeds. And a silver-haired woman stopped

dead on the trail. Her adult son held her upright,
her walker behind them. I thought, *When drought ends,*
rain will take one step towards green, then another.

I thought, *Soon the driest season must drown, one cloud*
broken, then another. A mile in, we glimpsed it—
grey-green, slow, carrying sludge and algae and snag,

but carrying on. Quiet. At the edge of an empire
shutting down, we stood a long time. The shallows
shuddering as a blue heron rose. Green vines

and willows on the far shore. After a while,
we turned back to the trail, back to the woman
and her son. Though not certain it was the same place

or a few steps further on. A little fear just behind
the temptation to go on exactly as we were.
After all, it was a glimpse of river lugged and choked,

but a river still. And these hours at day's end
conspiring towards belief—birdsong raining through
the cottonwoods, a sun so easily gold, gilding all.

After Learning the Transplant May Have Failed

How hurried the light after rain, the snow
geese wheeling across blue miles of wetlands,
the ponds sun-steeped gold in late afternoon.
If to pray is to ask and know there is no
one and nothing to answer, then
I will ask only to lie down in wet grass
wingless under this flyway, this vast sky
given to passage, I will ask please embed him
in the crossing over, please give my grandson
time in the only once of it. If to pray
is to plead, I will beg the dusk that worries
these wild flocks as they rise and fall
and cannot settle, will beg for him to stay
long among us, please it's late, hurry now.

Lullaby for the Sixth Extinction

In the purgatory of whatever paradise remains,
        I wait for my daughter's call

in my garden after rain, the sun a lit match
        held to the gas stove of spring,

daffodils sizzling yellow, the swell of tulips
        shoved through ground.

The future stalls, sends a violent ache
        into the beyond, our planet's next

apocalypse hanging in the air. Meanwhile
        I'm ready to burn carbon

100 miles to the hospital any day, at any hour,
        my grandson's mutated cells

multiplying alongside his small not-yets,
        his yes or no. Here,

wind stirs the grass around our pond, breeding
        mosquito fish, tiny frogs.

Deep in a world in limbo, beauty bewilders me.
        It's hard to love what may die

too soon. And yet time drags on, this baby thrown
        into civilization's cradle

rock-a-byeing on a bent and breaking bough.
        All of us repeating aloud,

It will be okay. Who wants to be the one to ask,
        And if it falls?

California Gold

Here, beside this creek choked
with algal bloom, it's the Maidu
wrapped in Sutter's blankets

that I can't stop thinking about.
How the women and children
lay down in rivers, on fire

with smallpox and fever
before they died. How gold
this light was then as now.

Sometimes I wish I didn't know
what this valley once was—
endless acres of wildflowers

under riparian oaks, rivers
packed so tight with salmon
you could walk across silvers

shore to shore. Now
it's star thistle and jimsonweed
erupting after drought.

And there, in the distance,
a vast field of sunflowers—
vegetal forest of stalks

heavy with bent platters. Gold
the eerie cheer of sunflowers
as they await the machinery's blades

that will sever their heads,
crush the seed into golden oil.
Gold rush at the source of it all.

And what lives on of slaughter,
how it makes a sound
like a question

wanting a different answer.
A sound like sticks
scratching on bone-dry ground.

Septic Shock

Because he's been working hard to stay alive,
my grandson's late to take his first steps,

say his first words (*more, dada, hi*), his hands
inventing a sideways wave for both bird and fish,

and he's so happy at home,
but then midnight, his parents race him to the ER,

the intensive care team shooting bolus after bolus
into his arteries shutting down, his mother

beside him, whispering, *It will be okay,* in tone
and touch, while the surgeon threads a tube

down his throat, pumps in breath, antibiotics,
sedatives, opiates, and he sways again

without us, between worlds. Five days
in septic shock, his blood poisoned

with infection. We watch his feet twitch,
his small chest lifted by the ventilator,

his spirit floating from one close invisibility
into another, into a nearly unbearable

argument, a *but, but* stammered to the beginning
we believed was promise, a universal seed.

After visiting hours, I leave the hospital
and a security guard smiles,

or not, everything’s blurred and off-kilter.
A baby is called into this world

and he’s supposed to stay a long time,
isn’t he?

Midsummer Argument with Fester and Rot

Early morning, and hot.
A starling chick silent in the road.

Gravity too solemn without song.
The fledgling fallen from her nest

onto asphalt, tossed into the bullseye
of the next eagle circling overhead.

Look away, I tell myself, *walk on*.
But I've turned back instead

to snap two giant leaves from the maples,
wrap the chick in a mildew-spotted, green shroud.

Not because of kindness, no. It is, at heart,
a bone I must pick with the nature of suffering.

With the terror I feel at the idea of God,
if that is how the starling mistakes me,

as I lift her into my palm,
carry her into the grotto's shade to die.

I'm sorry if this is all wrong,
I whisper to the fledgling.

Because who am I to mess
with the merciless machinery of this world?

Maybe this is the nature of suffering too.
The sorrow we've been asked to bear

without instruction on how to help.
Desolate, the echoing thud in my body

as the chick is soon to be taken from hers.
The world a wound the closer that you come.

Carrion, the song the starling will come to sing.
Always a darker lament below.

To My Best Friend Ten Years After His Suicide

Tonight I'm whispering to you
from the children's hospital,
the young men in their souped-up cars

burning wheelies on the street below,
your god-daughter's baby
in his metal crib. For close to a year,

we have watched the torment of his cure.
His rashes and fevers, his emptied,
writhing gut. Today he turned one,

and we sang "Happy Birthday" to him,
but he was too sick to care.
Do you remember down here on earth,

the constant assault of hurt and beauty?
How we both hated the sameness
of summer's ruthless heat?

Last night I dreamt the seas
were rising fast, and just before
a wave hit my house,

I felt you alive beside me
as rapture unharnessed from pain,
and I understood for the first time

why you had to go the way you did—
the body's difficult miracle
left, finally, far behind.

Behind the Fish Hatchery

We find them, two boys
barefoot among the blood
and iridescent spoils,
at summer's end,
the river rushing downhill,
salmon leaping up,
banging themselves fleshless
against the iron gates.

Already scores of dead
float along the shore,
ragged in the yellow reeds.
The smaller boy hops
and shrieks.
Not too close to the water,
the elder warns,
as he throws another
snagged Coho onto the ground.

If they were my boys,
would I say, *It's wrong to kill,*
or go on as I do
here beside them,
riding out the river's dark
and disappearing wild,
the older kid wrapping his hands
around the thrashing fish,
as he chokes it quiet now.

III.

Not all things are blest, but the seeds of all things are blest. The blessing is in the seed.

—Muriel Rukeyser

Aubade

This morning, time is a bridge you can cross.
Dolphins arc into black crescents
before they disappear

into the red-gold sea. Your old life
pried apart
and thrown down like prayer,

like these two white shells
hinged around empty
until there is only this light

that cuts and shines.
That honeys your breath
as it steams into air.

And water, its music against shore,
washing up sand dollars, crab shells,
a tobacco-colored jellyfish,

the hushed unknowable
as it blooms skeletal everywhere.
You wade into the cold shallows.

Even a moment without sadness
seems a long time. After lost,
after gone, finally it is now.

My Grandson's First Week Back in the World

Take the sky, swallowed down
by a warbler before it departs as song.

Or darkness steeping those first fourteen
months on the cancer floor in a white crib,

before the canopies of Chinese pistache
leak red across the horizon, the lemon trees

glowing in globes of juice. Today
we return to the garden with its forbidden

grass and soil, its bacteria and fungus
that, for too long, would have killed him.

But now, remade, maybe even cured,
he can be buckled into the swing's basket

where he flies, breathless, out and back,
over the strange crossings

he's been asked to make. Then we walk
to the sandbox under winter's lean scythe

of afternoon. Unstoppable, his want.
Look at how he starts, coating his hands,

his lips with dirt, his body finally anointed
with the lush possibilities of earth.

Pastoral Ache and Spire

Fields of barley and filaree.
A pool of oranges tipped from a semi
taking the corner too fast,

and beside it, bees drinking ditch water,
their buzz a humming in the dirt,
the rows of white hive boxes set out

in the almond orchard among the petals.
For no reason, we say when joy is inside us,
the holy spirit entering, if it does,

through the living spine of a tree
where I sit, my back against the bark.
A meadowlark drops musical notes

into the sound of a tractor spraying fields.
My husband has walked deep into shadows
laid down in orderly rows along the ground,

and whatever of me keeps following him
into that absence is oddly familiar,
the way a day like this works

against loneliness, against the choir
of sorrows inside an "I."
Like our grandson last week

stamping his feet, laughing
each time a red-winged blackbird
slipped from sky to lawn.

All of us in love with these months
outside the children's hospital,
though every hour holds its breath.

When my husband returns,
looking up at the lush canopy
above us, he asks,

What if there was no one to notice beauty?
The sublime inside his question,
and the ache about the end:

the human attention that makes
of the infinite a sliver small enough to hold.
Soon I'll teach my grandson

how to lace his hands together
with a spire risen up from two fingers,
while we chant, *Here's the church,*

here's the steeple—
as if a life is how we build a cage
around what passes through.

Six Months After He Leaves the Cancer Ward

I dream the rescue helicopter
lets me down near his overturned crib,
in the black vicinity of night.

Tethered to the whirring above,
I scan the waves for his small body,
too scared to swim out,

then awaken to a note from my daughter
that they're at the park.
How many times did I say it aloud,

that I'd gladly die if the baby lived?
Liar, promising something I can't give.
I mean, look at the possibilities

holding onto this morning under pear trees,
a tattooed couple kissing on a bench.
Nearby, a store displays blue pajamas

printed with yellow fish. Inside,
someone laughs, and turning, I catch
a teenage boy reaching for a mannequin's breast,

his friend instructing him how to properly
cup the plaster mound in his palm.
Seeing me, the boys blush.

One wears a nose-ring, eye make-up.
It's scary to be exactly who you are.
To believe you'll arrive into any future safely.

I'm afraid these pajamas are the last we have,
the clerk says. Small courage, I know
to hope. The only pair left

two sizes too large,
but like any prayer against death,
to buy them anyway.

Mud and Justice

You know how well it works to be told,
Don't think about it, he'll be fine,
while death lurks in the distance, silent

as the fireworks we watched, glassed-in,
from the top of the oncology pediatric ward,
where chemo burned my grandson,

thinned him to bone. Yet his first word, *More.*
You know how we want to believe
that whatever is torn from us

leaves behind a riverbed, waiting
to be filled again, and that it will come,
the reparative rain, gleaming like our boy

on his new legs climbing the garden steps,
saying, *More, more,* shattering us with his joy.
You know we don't get to choose

who we love, and maybe you know too,
how doubled is the going forward, the going
back, the way one threat recalls another,

how this morning, watching him lick
dark streaks of dirt on his hands,
I remember the mud I lay face down in

after the armed stranger was done.
You know there is a place inside us
that carries sadness for this world,

for death arriving at hello, my grandson's
little body dressed in a hospital gown
printed with rainbows. Of course

we want to believe babies don't endure
a year of chemo just to die,
or that rapists won't remain at large,

hunting in daylight, but the truth is,
justice is a lie. While mercy
is another story—as small

as how I remember best the bitter taste
of mud, not the gun at my temple,
not the stranger's weight against mine.

And mercy as large as that morning
I returned from the rape exam
to hold my infant daughter in my arms,

a flesh and bone joy in the face of death
working its way through time
like rain restoring the river's scar.

Laws of War

At the block party, old neighbors chatter around the bean dip.
It's warm in the street, a smoky light laid quietly everywhere.

This far in, we've learned the words for gone—
thirty years of ambulances whisking the eldest away—

while little by little, we've worked at joy,
how it holds a gun aimed at the cold silence of the stars.

Listen, the bullet says. And, *Yes and no.*
So we drink and laugh, while school-age kids kick a ball,

angling for the highest score. Down here
on this patch of dirt, I'd like to propose another law of war,

one that specifies how far from the front
we must carry the collateral damage with us,

especially into an evening like this,
happiness arming itself with the newest two-year-old,

dark curls, dark-eyed, in a white dress.
Unsmiling, it's dead serious,

how she wants me to watch her jump
as we stand on either side of time.

Above us, the elms touch, spreading their canopy
across the street into a bridal tent, and yes,

we must wed ourselves to each other
while we can, October's leaves staining red, falling faster now.

Human Time

Our grandson lies on his stomach, his forearms underwater,
trying to touch the flick and brush of mosquito fish,
the last koi to survive the heron's hunger.

Above us, the Sierras wait out another winter without snow.
Up there, the world can change its mind.
Can send down rain or heat for weeks, before the north winds

dust up carcinogens behind the farmers' plows.
Or simply leave the fields alone, purring with seed and song
and bone. All the bright glitter, I think,

the light inside the dirt. Always a little dark
with our grandson coming in at the end of day in my husband's arms,
their stone-cold hands smelling of wet leaves.

Tonight I twist an orange from our tree, under a shock of stars
driven into the vast abyss. Like I said, up there
the world can change its mind. Soon I'll slice the orange

into crescents to feed my grandson, juice glazing
his lips, his hands. Outside the spectacular brevity of human time,
deep calls to deep. Sweet, with a bite from the other side.

To My Stillborn as a Sonnet

Inside the orchard where the shadow of the birds
passed through me as a new mother, I remember
the sweet-crisp of a just-picked Jonathan.
A heron arrowing dark across the canal.
Back then, I believed that what I saw came to you
like a larger eye opening over a meadow.
That if you hadn't died before you were born,
I'd never know sorrow or restlessness. Now
I'm old enough to see that when I don't move,
the swallows come most alive. They sweep over
cattails, commune in high flute through an afternoon.
This close to the end, it's plain how it hurts
and heals at once, this earthly beauty before
it's erased. How death only asks for everything.

When He Says He's a Bird, He Can Go So High

even now that he's been stolen back   his grandfather & I
are quiet before what passes   unspoken   from the almost-not
of this child's first year   that next world   seamed too close
& gleaming   as I read to him about a finch   perched in a pine
Good night   the forest says to him   though I'm still listening
to the absence   of ICU alarms & monitors   in his not-yet-taken
tomorrow   where he ran today   scaring up ravens   starlings
forcing them like buds   to open their wings   into the spirit world
that we've named sky   listen   all songbirds are oscines
from the order *Passeri*   & they perch a lifetime here   listen
finch   sparrow   pine siskin   I'm not asking   for the never-
ending   I just want to call him *Little Passerine*   as if
I believe it   that he has permission to stay   for the whole story

Coda with Bird and Paper Lantern

Before she died, my mother told me
I could do anything. So I've taught
myself to fly in dreams.

You need only a downward slope,
a running start, your arms held out like wings.
The lift is easy, the steering hard.

I often slam my head against arches,
a hidden casement, a ceiling fan
before I reach the sky.

The way we thought my grandson
would be snuffed out by chemo, by the cancer
in his blood, before he was a year old.

Wake up! he loves to say now. *Wake up!*
Today he hit me because I wouldn't let him
stand alone in the street.

Luckily he's easy to distract.
I showed him two fish drawn
on the sidewalk.

They looked as if they were flying
above concrete. *See,* I pointed
and he used this sideways wave

he invented to say *fish.*
As well as *bird.*
Because language is like flying too.

How it can carry you
away from loneliness.
These days my grandson is an ecstatic.

His body a whirl of motion
until bed,
where he cries himself to sleep.

It goes so fast, enjoy it while you can,
everyone tells my daughter.
Wake up, wake up, I think.

His cancer broke us into different
things. For me, a bird at night,
that doesn't remember how to rise

without hitting itself hard
on the way out. For my daughter,
a paper lantern carrying flame

she knows to set in water,
alive and burning however long
it lasts, however far it goes.

Notes

Lullaby for the Sixth Extinction
The title refers to the fact that although our planet has been through five previous events of mass extinction, the current apocalyptic challenges to plants, animals, oceans, and landforms are not caused by natural phenomena, but instead are driven by human activity.

"Human Time," p. 33 *Deep calls to deep* is taken from Psalm 42:7, with thanks to Suzanne Edison.

Acknowledgments

"After Learning the Transplant May Have Failed," "Coda with Bird and Paper Lantern," "If Math Might Hold the Terror Down," "Midsummer Fester and Rot," "Mud and Justice," "The Second Coming," *Calul Journal*, July 20, 2025.

"Almond Orchard in Blossom," *Sacramento Poetry Center News*, November 2024.

"Behind the Fish Hatchery," *Sacramento Poetry Center News*, March 2024.

"Children's Oncology Ward" appeared in *The Missouri Review*, Poem of the Week, July 2023, and was a finalist for the 2023 Perkoff Prize. Awarded a Pushcart Prize, this poem was reprinted in *Pushcart Prize XLIX* (2025).

"His First Week Back in the World," *The Baltimore Review*, 2024.

"How it Begins," *SWIIM,* January 2024.

"Infant Leukemia," "Little Vamp," "On the Carrizo Plains," and "Easier Said Than Done" appeared as a single poem titled "Catalog of Infant Leukemia" in *The Hippocrates Initiative for Poetry and Medicine, 2024 Award-Winners Anthology.*

"Inventory of Infant Leukemia," *The Southern Review,* Winter 2024.

"Laws of War," *Blackbird,* June 2025.

"Lullaby for the Sixth Extinction," LIMINAL SPACES, 2025.

"Milk" was originally published in *The Southern Review,* Winter 2022, and was republished in *Verse Daily*, as well as in *Attached to the Living World, A New Eco-Poetry Anthology,* Eds., Ann Fisher-Wirth and Laura-Gray Street (Trinity University/Terra Firma, 2025).

"Septic Shock," *MER Medical Motherhood Folio*, September 2024.

"Stages of Grief" and "Too Late Pastoral," *Terrain*, March 2024.

Thank you to my brilliant community of poets who helped me with these poems in revision, but even more, in holding faith in writing: Kelli Russell Agodon, Ellery Akers, Idris Anderson, Susan Browne, Beverly Burch, Susan Cohen, Suzanne Edison, Gerald Fleming, Rebecca Foust, George Higgins, Matthew Lippman, Joseph Millar, Zach Rogow, Eliot Schain, Murray Silverstein, Robert Thomas, Jeanne Wagner, and Steven Winn. Also, to my beloved family, especially Sophie and Rob for allowing me to work in the only way I could with the events related to our newest family member. To Nancy Botkin for choosing my manuscript for the publication prize, and to Joseph Chaney, along with Nancy Botkin, who shepherded this collection into a book.

And always, always, to Steve.

About the Author

Julia B. Levine's recent poetry awards include the 2015 Northern California Book Award for her fourth collection, *Small Disasters Seen in Sunlight* (LSU 2014), a 2024 Pushcart Prize, the 2024 *Terrain* Poetry Prize, the 2023 Oran Robert Perry Burke Award from *The Southern Review*, as well as a 2022 Academy of American Poets Laureate Fellowship for her work in building resiliency in teenagers in the context of climate change. Her work has appeared in *Ploughshares, The Nation, The Southern Review, The Missouri Review*, and *Prairie Schooner*. She earned a PhD from University of California, Berkeley, and an MFA in poetry from Pacific University. Her fifth collection, *Ordinary Psalms* (LSU 2021), won a Nautilus Silver Award in Poetry.

sites.google.com/view/juliablevine

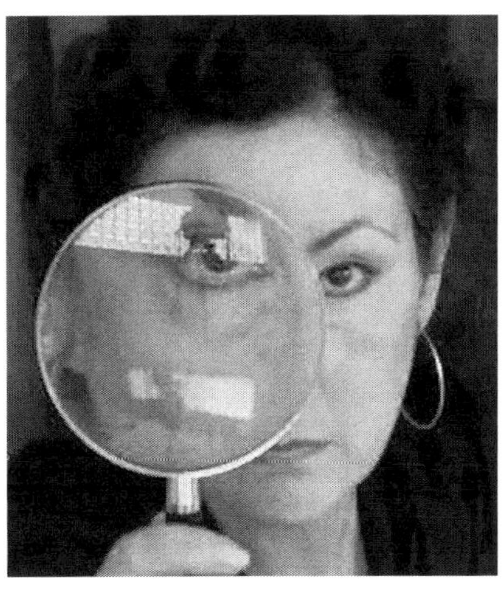

About the Cover Artist

Carolyn Zacharias McAdams was born and raised in north Texas. She has a BFA in Drawing and Painting from the University of North Texas in Denton. She was awarded the Medal of Honor from the National Association of Women Artists, Inc., and was one of five finalists for "featured artists" in the Texas Biennial 2009. Her art is featured in *The Southern Review* (Winter 2025). McAdams is represented by Craighead Green Gallery, Dallas, and LeMieux Galleries in New Orleans. She lives and works with two cats in Denton, Texas.

Follow Carolyn on Instagram: https://www.instagram.com/artsnotfunny/

https://www.craigheadgreen.com/
https://lemieuxgalleries.com/artist/carolyn-zacharias-mcadams

Artist Statement

I am a storyteller whose narratives are expressed in images instead of words. At an early age, viewing my father's work (photographic portraits), I realized the power of emotion portrayed simply by light, composition, and staging. This meant I could tell my tales without saying a word. I have spent long hours looking at stained glass windows in Catholic churches, further informing my ideas of metaphor and story. These windows still influence my palette—pure colors directly from the tube that are mixed but rarely muted. Fascinated by more intimate forms of art (jewelry, doll houses, illuminated manuscripts), I found that the details and precision inspired me to work in a small scale. I want each piece to be seen as simultaneously delicate and bold. The imagery of my work is an outward display of thoughts, dreams, anxieties, and fears. I begin a piece with no plan, no theme, no sketches. I simply start painting, and through "stream of consciousness," I let the process direct the next steps. This keeps the work exciting for me. I am always surprised by what comes through. These little narratives generally include animals, especially cats and birds. I've always imagined stories in my mind about what animals are thinking and doing, and their attitudes and gestures are a large part of my fantasies and dreams. The landscape creates mood and a sense of place that becomes the backdrop as well as an integral part of the story.

The paintings have no beginning and no end. They are each a part of the same story, changing with time yet always connected.

Carolyn Zacharias McAdams